GET-REAL LEADERSHIP

A Practical Approach That Delivers Relationships, Respect *and* Results

HARRY S. CAMPBELL

D1468690

Praise for <u>Get-Real Leadership</u>

"It's always a joy to learn important life and career-enhancing wisdom from someone like Harry, who has achieved such phenomenal success. What makes this an even greater experience is that he shows us how to do it in a way that is easy to grasp. The lessons, the stories, the principles...they make such great sense. If you are a leader or want to be one, this book is for you. If you have a son or daughter whom you would like to equip with the skills they need to one day be a leader, this book is for them. Terrific, terrific book!"

— **Bob Burg, Coauthor**
The Go-Giver* and *It's Not About You

"Harry brings an endless supply of enthusiasm, positive energy, curiosity and humility to everything he does. He has captured the essence of those characteristics in <u>Get-Real Leadership</u>. Anyone in a leadership role can benefit from this book through Harry's straightforward focus on sincerity, empathy, competitive fire, and above all, a relentless commitment to being genuine in all aspects of work and life."

— **Clay Herron, Chief Financial Officer**
Olympus Media, LLC

Praise for <u>Get-Real Leadership</u>

"Read this book only if you're serious about positive change in your career and life. While many concepts appear to be simple at first glance, living them will test you – and ultimately force you to decide who you really are."

— **Patrick S. O'Brien**
Author, *Making College Count*

"The greatest challenge for managers is to provide honest and constructive feedback. Harry's <u>Get-Real Leadership</u> drives home the point why so many of us struggle. It's hard to do something well if you don't allow yourself the freedom of being your *real* self while you do it!"

— **Mark Guinan, Chief Financial Officer**
Hill-Rom Medical Equipment

"From the cover to the last page...this is clearly one of the most authentic books I've read on leadership. Harry Campbell's honest reflection in <u>Get Real Leadership</u> on his own highly successful "real life" career reminds us all that we have just one life—comprised of work, and play, and family, and every other aspect of how we live. An insightful learning for all current and future leaders."

— **Matt Anthony, Global Chairman**
VML

From Harry's Team

"Harry's energy, passion and humility shine through as if he's telling his story over a cup of coffee. In a world of corporate politics, cut-throat competition and jargon, his approach to Get-Real Leadership is a breath of fresh air. He proves that you can get results – and respect – without sacrificing relationships or personal priorities. It's all about being real."

— **Maria Fogliasso, Social Media Manager**

"This book is as charismatic and inspirational as Harry Campbell himself!"

— **Valerie Sabbarese, Call Center Supervisor**

"Great leaders inspire their people to deliver extraordinary results. Campbell is a real leader, true to himself and his people."

— **David Cordisco, Director Retail Sales**

"I've had the opportunity to work for many knowledgeable leaders, but it wasn't until Harry that I saw what it truly meant to lead, not just put out unreal expectations and demand they be accomplished."

— **Troy Nickerson, Retail Store Manager**

From Harry's Team

"Harry brought new life and focus to the teams he worked with at my company – his servant leadership was evident in every interaction and decision he made. The man walks the walk."

— **Erin Rasmus, Senior Product Manager**

"I was more motivated in the two hours I just spent reading this book than I have been at the past three leadership conferences I have attended."

— **Tyra Kendall, Retail Store Manager**

"From my first meeting with Harry I knew I had found a very special leader. So, the next day I left a job paying $25K more because I knew that what I could learn from him would return more throughout my lifetime. He's for real."

— **Lisa Platt, Retail Store Manager**

"You have to love an executive that tells you how it is, doesn't sugar coat, and even uses expletives because of his own excitement. Harry Campbell is a true original!"

— **Denise Myers, Senior Marketing Manager**

Proceeds from <u>Get-Real Leadership</u>

Harry S. Campbell's <u>Get-Real Leadership</u> book sales and speaking engagements will benefit the *Head for the Cure Foundation* to find a cure for brain cancer.

In October 2003, Harry and his wife Kris registered for the inaugural *Head for the Cure – Metro KC* 5K to support the Anthony family. Neither suspected brain cancer would affect their immediate family just four months later.

Kris was diagnosed in February 2004, at age 34, with a grade II astrocytoma brain tumor. Although her tumor has been slow-growing, it is a malignant form of brain cancer and her tumor has proved to be inoperable.

The Campbells, along with their family and friends, have funneled their fundraising and awareness efforts into *Head for the Cure* through "Team Kris Campbell." Consistently a top team in fundraising and participation, "Team Kris Campbell" has raised over $160,000 since 2004 and recruits 150 to 250 walkers, runners, and strollers for the annual *Head for the Cure – Metro KC* 5K.

To support "Team Kris Campbell," please visit: **www.headforthecure.org/teamkriscampbell**.

Proceeds from <u>Get-Real Leadership</u>

About Head for the Cure

The *Head for the Cure Foundation* is a 501(c)(3) nonprofit organization dedicated to raising awareness and funding in the fight against brain cancer.

Head for the Cure is committed to providing ongoing financial support to programs including the Brain Tumor Trials Collaborative (BTTC), a network of NCI-accredited medical centers, led by MD Anderson, with the expertise and the desire to participate in state-of-the-art clinical trials investigating new treatments for malignant brain tumors.

Members of "Team Kris Campbell"
August 2011

GET-REAL LEADERSHIP

❖ ❖ ❖ ❖ ❖

Dedication

With love to the four who give me strength, hope and joy,

my wife Kris and my children

Harrison, Madeleine and Matthew.

You bless me.

❖ ❖ ❖ ❖ ❖

Contents

Foreword

When I pick up a book on leadership, I don't look first at the *Table of Contents*, or the endorsements on the back cover. I head straight for the author bio because I'm more interested in *who* than *how* when it comes to leading.

Here's what I mean. I count mountain-climbing among my hobbies, but don't ask me to take on Mount Everest with help from a winsome guide loaded with pricey gear who has googled a few tips, then points me to the top with a promise to cheer loudly as I climb. No, give me the man or woman who has made it to the top and on the way maybe dangled over the edge of a cliff or two – and survived. I want guidance that comes from experience. I'm betting you do, too.

The same is true as I think about business. Anyone can slap on a leadership label and deliver an instructive – maybe even a compelling – story of how others should be managed. But I want to learn from someone who's been proven.

When I met Harry Campbell a couple of years ago as he participated in the Goalden Eagle Coaching Program I lead for senior-level executives, I recognized he knew how to win at business.

He'd just come from an executive role in his third Fortune 500 company, and in each of those positions, the teams he led had been wildly successful.

What I later discovered, though, was the deeper, more important part of Harry. Unlike some other leaders who produced like he did, Harry's people were wild about him. And crazy about working in his organization, enough so that he had more wanting to move from other parts of the company to his business unit than he could handle.

As I got to know him, I found out why. Harry combines integrity and passion in a way that makes the word "authentic" sound like it was invented to describe him.

In a success celebration during one of his business cycles, his people gifted him with an enormous scroll on which were printed email messages of appreciation and respect from hundreds of employees. By far the most common praise? "Harry, we trust you because *you're real*..."

Harry Campbell gets it. He's taken the concept of Servant Leadership and makes that concept the operational principle for the way he makes money and makes work a great place for all.

I'm grateful Harry has chosen to share what he knows about Get-Real Leadership. Through his openness and experiences, you'll find in the pages ahead a clearly marked path to winning at work and at the same time being blisteringly true to yourself.

Dr. Tom Hill, Ed.D.
St. Louis, MO

❖ ❖ ❖ ❖ ❖

A Note from the Author

Over the past couple of decades, I have met quite a few leaders who touted books about their successes. I often rolled my eyes (discreetly, of course) and sometimes muttered to myself, "He thinks he's created a foolproof formula for success and if I'd just read his book and follow his lead, I might have a crack at success, too."

How ironic that I now find myself coming to you with a book in hand!

For me, the impetus to capture my thoughts on leadership didn't start with an inflated sense of grandeur. After all, I have two teenagers; therefore I technically know *nothing*! Instead, I decided to write this as a way to say "thank you."

I've been in business more than twenty-five years and been blessed to lead in several Fortune 500 companies and small businesses. In these roles, I've been successful in ways that surprised many, including me!

For me, the most important part of the success wasn't the titles or the status or the money. It was – and is – the relationships with the people I worked with.

Meeting them in the office or on the street was – and is – joyful since these are the folks I care about, trust and respect. The cool thing is I often sense the feeling is mutual.

Knowing how to create rich, authentic relationships while functioning as a winning team – that was my dream as a young leader. But when I looked around, I saw few models to follow. Many of those in senior positions were more concerned about their careers or the company's success than they were about how they treated people or how we approached the business at hand. This seemed off to me.

Fortunately, I had other sources of input. There were positive role models – like Sam Walton of Walmart fame, who demonstrated to a young manager how to lead others with integrity and respect while still producing winning results. To these leaders I owe a deep debt of gratitude.

It occurred to me that one way to say thanks was to help others live out what these leaders had inspired in a liberal arts major from a small town in southern Indiana. So, with this end in mind, the idea of a book was born.

I have a second, even more personal purpose, and it is unashamedly connected to money.

Just before our first wedding anniversary in 2004, my wife Kris was diagnosed with a malignant brain tumor which we would later learn was inoperable.

By great grace the tumor is slow growing, so we receive each day as the gift that it is, making the most of all we've been given.

Besides living life fully, our other focus is working toward a cure for this disease. To that end, we are passionate in supporting *Head for the Cure*, a wonderful non-profit organization committed to helping find a cure for brain cancer. If you purchased this book, please know all the proceeds, and the proceeds from my speaking engagements on Get-Real Leadership, go to *Head for the Cure*.

If you'd like to help further or find out more, please visit the "Team Kris Campbell" page on the *Head for the Cure* website: **www.headforthecure.org/teamkriscampbell**.

So, driven by gratitude for those that showed me the way and a desire to help a cause that matters deeply to our family, I dove into capturing my thoughts on leadership.

I trust that the time you are investing to explore these ideas will increase your own courage and commitment to leading with authenticity and caring. And someday, I expect to be reading *your* book about what you learned as you made Get-Real Leadership your own.

Harry S. Campbell
Overland Park, KS

GET-REAL LEADERSHIP

1

What Get-Real Leadership Can Do For You

- The deal-breaking dilemma every leader must resolve
- How the richest man in the world showed a way out
- Why Get-Real Leadership can lead to wild success without sacrificing your authentic self

I arrived at Procter & Gamble (P&G) at age 23 with an MBA in Marketing. However, once I took on more leadership in my department, I quickly realized there were critical questions about how business *really* worked that my MBA program had failed to cover.

I saw some cutthroat people around me drive impressive business results—and get promotions as a result. I also saw some of the more people-focused leaders get passed over.

I saw political players who became someone different when the Big Boss came into the room, squelching their real selves to create a "promotable presence." Some of leaders who didn't act the part paid a price in promotability.

Successful as a results-driver, or successful in making P&G a great place to work for employees? Successful as a "company man," or successful in being true to my personality? I could see rewards and issues with each. Choices would need to be made.

Of course I was 23 and had plenty on my plate. I likely would have allowed leadership style decisions to take a backseat to learning how to make a buck if two unexpected and challenging interventions hadn't occurred.

The first challenge

As part of a leadership development program, we were asked to take the Herrmann Brain Dominance Instrument assessment. We would then get a read-out from a Herrmann coach. Sounded interesting, and kind of fun; that is, until I got my results.

As the coach and I sat together reviewing the feedback, she shook her head. "You have to know," she told me, "I've rarely seen a profile like yours."

I didn't know whether she meant this as a compliment or a critique, so I decided to wait for the explanation before reacting. I had scored about as high as possible on two dimensions, she explained. Fine, I always liked bringing in high scores. The problem was that these two dimensions were polar opposites.

"You're nearly as high as you can be in valuing relationships and driving for significant and inspirational relationships with people," she told me. So far, I didn't see a problem.

"But your scores are even higher on buckling down and producing like crazy against business goals. In fact, in this dimension, you scored outside our normative 'box.'

"You are top-tier competitive—the kind that cannot bear to lose—but also top-tier relationship—the kind that can't bear to win unless you win 'with.' It probably feels like there's a raging battle going on inside your head whether to kick the crap out of a competitor to win, or to invite them to go out for a beer. The tension in making everyday decisions will be enormous until you resolve these two powerful pulls."

Actually, she'd described me to a "T." I was new to leadership, but already I was plagued with uncertainty about decisions when it appeared I had to choose between treating people well and hitting our numbers.

The second challenge

I performed well as assistant brand manager for Pepto-Bismol, helping introduce the largest line extension in the history of the brand, and in a couple of years I was ready for a promotion. P&G offered a couple of options. The first involved moving to Osaka, Japan, to lead a large brand. The second was a move to Bentonville, Arkansas, to be part of the formation/development of a joint P&G-Walmart customer business team charged with revolutionizing the way packaged goods go to market.

People around me questioned my sanity when I chose Arkansas over Osaka. This was 1988, and for corporate up-and-comers, having an international assignment under your belt was critical to a pathway for promotion. But the word "revolutionize" in the job description sounded interesting, and Walmart founder Sam Walton had just been identified as the richest man in the world. I was pretty sure there'd be things to learn there, so I headed south.

As it turned out, that two-and–a-half-year stint in the land of the Razorbacks provided the fodder I was seeking to design a leadership model that would guide me for decades.

First, I knew how phenomenally successful Walmart had become under Sam Walton, and if I paid attention to what I saw and heard about their operating style and philosophy, I'd be growing as a competitor in the marketplace.

It turned out I was right about learning business savvy. I still apply lessons from those days in my business planning. For instance, at one point I met David Glass, CEO of Walmart, at a trade show.

I asked him what they were going to do to beat Kmart, which was at that time their major competitor. What Mr. Glass said has stuck with me to this day. He said it wasn't one big thing; it was the hundreds of little things they did better than competitors like Kmart. "If it was one big thing we did extremely well," he explained, "someone would figure it out, find a way to do it better, and our days in the front of the pack would be over. Instead it is the accumulation of those hundreds of little things that enables us to win."

Business ideas like these served me well.

But it wasn't long before I understood Walton's leadership had more than a keen understanding of how to compete unrelentingly for profits.

The first day I walked into the Walmart corporate offices, I faced a wall with letters three feet high that said, "Servant Leaders." Under these words were the names of the senior executive team.

I soon learned that Walton didn't just mouth the rhetoric of leaders valuing their employees. I heard he had told a senior leader who worked for him, "It's not your employees' job to make your job easier; it's *your* job to make *their* jobs easier. If you can't find a way to do that, you don't belong here."

I thought at once about the assessment I'd taken that had left me in a quandary. Here was the richest man in the world who had built a company from a small storefront into a global powerhouse—and he also was committed to treating employees well. Indeed, serving them. Profits and people. I was hearing the language of both here.

Putting pieces together

The most powerful experience came for me as I learned more about Walton's lifestyle.

I'd just left P&G headquarters, remember, and knew first-hand what the lifestyle of an executive looked like.

Expansive offices with their own bathrooms and personal conference rooms, outfitted with lots of glass and mahogany. The executive parking garage, travel on the corporate jet, amazing homes in the wealthiest part of the city. The best of everything.

I soon learned these things weren't part of Walton's way. He drove an old brown pickup instead of a luxury car and his modest office in "executive row" at the Walmart headquarters sported a metal desk.

Once on a flight out of Bentonville, I wound up sitting by Mrs. Walton. (Sam Walton's wife flew commercial? I couldn't believe it!)

She was, well, just so nice to me. Asked me questions, chatted as comfortably as if she was really interested in this 27-year-old kid who wasn't even officially a part of the Walmart Team. In other words, she didn't have to be nice to me.

Another time, at a charity event, I wound up standing next to Mr. Walton and decided to show off my $8 Walmart watch. He grinned, then showed me his watch, which cost less than mine because it had been on sale.

I was amazed to find that the Waltons were, it seemed to me, people who were simply "real."

Could I be successful and still respect myself?

These observations impacted me so deeply that after a few years in a large corporation, I was already beginning to feel conflicted about how much of myself to reveal at work. I could look around and see who was getting promotions. Most were more staid than I was, more careful about what they said, less quick to joke, more quick to espouse the business line. They often ate at the right restaurants, drove the right cars, and worried over the most visible positioning of their desks or office space.

These things did not interest me as places to invest energy, but my competitive side wondered if I was making a mistake by not being more appearance conscious. Would I become labeled too goofy or too quirky to be considered for upper management at P&G? Would I need to cover parts of my personality at work in order to succeed?

The Get-Real Leadership solution

Though I was sure I would not lead in exactly the same way Sam Walton had, the time in Northwest Arkansas showed me a way to respect both profits and people in the way I led by choosing to Get Real. Here's how I framed it.

To *Get Real with myself* by knowing who I am and what I stand for—and operating by those values.

To *Get Real with people* by inspiring them with optimism, respect, and caring.

To *Get Real about business* by becoming the most results-driven and competitive business leader I could, and by creating profitability in seemingly impossible situations.

In the years that followed, these three principles formed my framework of Get-Real Leadership.

Outcomes

It's now two decades post-P&G, and I've had opportunities to apply this brand of leadership in management and then senior executive positions in two other Fortune 500 companies, and also in a small but rambunctious marketing agency and an internet start-up.

I can tell you from experience, Get-Real Leadership works in all settings—when financial targets are $200,000 and when they're $2 billion. When your employees number 30 and when they number 100 times that. When your company is privately owned and when it's publicly traded. When you're in a "hot" tech-based industry and when you're in a stodgy, declining industry like wire-line telephone.

By "it works" I mean this: You can lead business units both small and large to exceed financial expectations— good times and bad, recessions or no.

But more importantly, when you get feedback from employees about your work together, the thing they will most often say is that they trusted you because you were real.

Get-Real is for those who want to "win anyway"

One of my managers explained it when he evaluated our time working together this way:

"There are a lot of us who see that the other side is cheating. Many of the other managers and executives around us are okay with leaving a wake of destruction, by manipulating people and putting themselves first. Cheating! And we see them succeeding at it—getting promotions, making lots of money, quoted in magazines, and being revered for their triumphs.

"I don't want to have to emulate some of the ruthless, political executives I've seen, but I don't want to have to settle for second place! I want to be a good guy and still win. However, it's tough to win against a team that's not playing fair. It will take a lot of extra hard work, lots of practice, smart plays, and adaptability.

"You're the experienced coach who has done the right thing and still had a winning season. You're putting your arm around younger leaders who want to play fair, helping them see what they're up against, and teaching them what they need to do to win anyway."

That's what I'd like to do for you in the pages ahead.

What this book won't do for you, and what it will

If you are looking for a book that tells you to dream big dreams as your path to success, this isn't it.

However, if you're looking for a practical, doable way to lead people that will let you help them enthusiastically give their best while consistently churning out winning results, this is the place for you.

Relationships. Respect. Results. That's Get-Real Leadership. Ahead we'll explore how it works and how it can work for you, starting with how you lead the toughest person you'll ever have to manage—yourself.

PART ONE
GET REAL WITH YOURSELF

"Be who you are and say what you feel because those who mind don't matter and those who matter don't mind."

— **Dr. Seuss**

2

Create Your Brand

- Using personal branding to Get Real about yourself
- The process of discovering a personal brand
- Validating your personal brand

At Procter & Gamble, branding wasn't just a marketing gimmick or the name for a product. The product's brand actually *was* the product.

Here's what I mean.

About two years into my time there, one of my peers working on Scope mouthwash came up with what looked on the surface to be a creative idea to make more profit.

The plant that produced Scope had excess capacity that could be used effectively. In other words, with only a small investment on P&G's part, the factory could have been producing a whole lot more mouthwash.

31

Why not produce mouthwash for someone else—maybe a generic brand? My counterpart developed a great business case, comparing the needed investment to the potential profitability. The numbers looked great, so he presented it to a senior executive for consideration.

The P&G senior executive took one look at the idea, and then glowered at the young marketing assistant. He spat out, "You have completely missed the point. We do not make mouthwash: WE MAKE SCOPE! Get out of my office and come up with plans to sell more SCOPE and beat the competition!"

Everyone who was in the room and who heard the story got the point. Brand is a big deal around P&G.

This resulted in a "teaching moment" for me. I realized I had not solidified what I wanted my personal brand to be. I was seriously wrestling with *the kill 'em to win vs. love 'em to be respected* dilemma. What was true for me, anyway? If I was to be authentic in the workplace, what was I going to stand for?

Personal branding as a path to authenticity

It became apparent to me that what I was learning as a marketing manager about branding could provide a path to identify what was real for me.

- A great brand has to differentiate, and, since no two people are alike, if my personal definition didn't somehow set me apart, I probably hadn't arrived at the right definition.

- A lasting brand keeps its promise, and "walking the talk" was my definition of personal authenticity.

- A solid brand had to be validated by the product's customers, not just an internal team, and I knew already that if my team didn't experience my leadership the way I defined it, something was wrong.

If Harry Campbell was a product, what would his brand be? I devised a way to find out. The result has stayed with me for nearly a quarter century, so I know from experience that this process works. Since then, I've shared my personal brand with thousands of others. I firmly believe they've found it a useful way to get to know me quickly, and they've found this process a way to develop a solid picture of their personal brands.

Discovering your personal brand
So, how to go about discovering—or maybe uncovering—what's most real about you?

I started with a solid marketing principle from my MBA days: others are better judges of an advertising campaign than the campaign's creator is. Indeed, the very act of creation requires such a personal investment and commitment, it becomes nearly impossible to step outside ourselves and see what actually is working and what isn't.

Soliciting input from others is a critical part of finding your brand.

A seven-word reality check

I applied this principle and came up with a simple way to find out what others would say about me. I approached a number of people and asked them what seven words most accurately would let others know who Harry Campbell is and what they can expect when they relate to him.

I made it clear I wasn't looking for a seven-word phrase ("Friendly and funny with a killer instinct"), but rather seven individual words. I chose to ask for seven because I found as I experimented with the process, I could describe people fairly easily in three or four words. It was when I had to determine the final 3-4 that I started to sweat, and the description became harder and thus more enlightening.

I also asked for this feedback to be delivered *anonymously*, which meant the feedback had to go to a third-party they could trust would compile it and not disclose who said what.

Without this provision for anonymity, our natural tendency to spare others' feelings will usually overwhelm the nuances of honesty, especially if the people providing feedback care about us personally and about continuing the relationship. Or, in the case of direct reports, anonymity is critical to ensure that you're not just being fed what they think you want to hear about yourself.

It's important to ask people you trust and who know you well. However, it's also useful to include some who aren't as close, and even those you believe aren't as crazy about you as, say, your mother is.

The deciding issue isn't about who likes you or doesn't. You'll choose by looking at how you intend to use what you learn. Whose feedback will best help you make more confident decisions about what's real for you?

Validating your brand

Of course, while others are creating their feedback, you need to do this exercise for yourself, too. In other words, you'll be creating your own list of seven words that you believe accurately describes you.

Then the feedback you receive will either reinforce that you've come to a fairly accurate understanding of yourself or generate healthy questions, either about your self-perception, or about how you communicate with the rest of the world.

At this point, neither their view nor yours is the "right" one. We're looking for a balanced go-forward way to define what's real for you and bring it into your leadership style.

Pay attention to the gaps

There may be no differences in the two descriptions. If so, congratulations. You know what's real for you, and you've been living out that reality in a way that others can see. If this is the case for you, you can move right onto learning ways to share your brand more effectively and use it to drive soul-confirming success.

If there are gaps, ask yourself what happened? What are they? How big are they? Why might they exist? Are you kidding yourself about who you really are? (For example, I see myself as incredibly funny. You'd be amazed at how differently my teenage kids describe my sense of humor. Go figure.)

Significant gaps might suggest a need to seek help to understand what's going on.

From the outcome of this branding exercise, you want to move confidently into honest and consistent use of what's real for you in personal and business decision-making.

You can't have that confidence if you're starting from a shaky foundation. Plus, you may find the process of understanding the gap will give you powerful insights.

I had this experience and came away the better for it. When I first defined my brand, I didn't include "impatient." I had convinced myself that I was merely driven and not impatient. Well, the outside world let me know this was not the case. Virtually all included "impatient" in their description of my personal brand. I wasn't particularly pleased with this, but felt I had to embrace it—and still do — as one of my brand attributes since it was so real to others.

Making real **more** *real*

Remember in this process, that even though we're using a corporate marketing technique to capture a self-definition, this can't be marketing gimmick. Here's what I mean. Materialism and status don't mean much to me, so I live in ways that are sometimes inconsistent with what many people expect from someone who has done the jobs I've had.

For instance, when I worked at Sprint and Embarq, at lunchtime I'd often leave my office and run across the street to Taco Bell. Heck of a deal, from my view. For under $5, I could get a meal and watch ESPN for a half hour with no distractions.

Also, I drive a RAV4, which is not exactly a pricey status car. Not that there's anything wrong with having a BMW or Mercedes; cars just don't matter to me, so I don't see them as a satisfying place to spend money. And when I traveled to our call centers or retail stores, I'd go without the entourage that many senior execs seem to collect. I'd just grab my briefcase and show up.

I learned that these choices were a huge hit with employees and seemed to move them toward trusting me as a leader who could identify with them and their lives. However, I did not make these choices to create the impression that I was an approachable or humble leader. That kind of manipulation is the opposite of Get-Real Leadership.

One employee told me, "Someone I used to work for was told he should get more involved with employees, so he scheduled an individual talk with one of us once a week. However, it was pretty clear being with him he didn't care one way or the other what we said in the conversation, and he did nothing with the ideas we offered.

"He should have saved himself some time because his 'I Care' program only convinced us that he truly didn't care."

I think you understand the caution I'm offering. Personal branding shouldn't be a PR campaign to make you popular. It's designed to help you be authentic.

Now, with this personal baseline established, we'll look at intentional, reasonable, useful ways to share your brand—in other words, to share yourself.

3

Share Your Brand

- Capture your brand in seven words
- Find a comfortable format to share your brand
- You don't have to share *everything*

It's the early introductions and commitments we make to our people that let them know what to expect of us. Because that's true, I often start out with new teams by telling them about my academic and professional journey, so they have a sense of where I came from and what I've done. I considered it an icebreaker and a credibility builder, and I still do.

However, after I began understanding the idea of personal branding, it occurred to me that sharing my brand with new teams would be a good way to let them know more than just what was on my resume.

In the new relationship we were establishing, it could be a way for me to go first, to let them know more of who I am and what matters to me. I thought it might also show a possible method for them to let me know who they were. Sort of a relationship-starter, if you will.

So I took my seven words, and to lighten it up a bit (as well as to personalize the story even more), I added a logo to each word. You may do this differently, but I'm offering the presentation I most often use with new employee groups as a way to provoke a design for your own use.

Here's the result: Harry's brand in seven words:

❖ Team-oriented

I'm as fanatical an Indiana Hoosiers fan as there is, but that isn't the reason I'm topping my list of what matters to me with their logo. In Hoosiers basketball, you won't see players' names on the back of their jerseys; they win or lose as a team. In work and life it's about teamwork for me. We are in this together.

❖ Positive (Attitude, attitude, attitude!)

If you hang around me for any period of time, you'll hear about my time at Procter & Gamble as Brand Manager of Metamucil.

That team and I learned together that if you can be aggressively proud about selling a remedy for constipation, you can be positive about most anything! A positive attitude wins, in business and in life.

❖ Tenacious

I am one tenacious SOB. I hate to lose, and I never, ever give up.

In high school I wanted desperately to be good at sports, but for most of the sports offered, I didn't have the skills to excel. Then I found long-distance running. Cross-country required a little skill and a lot of putting one foot in front of the other. That I could do.

At Vanderbilt I set the school record for the 10,000 meters in the spring of 1982, a record that still stands three decades later. That accomplishment is one I talk about proudly, because it reminds me you don't have to show up as the smartest or most talented or best connected. You can get there—and even get there first—by just sticking with it.

❖ Optimistic

I must be a serious optimist, because I am a Cubs fan. Every year when spring training comes around, we Cubs fans come up with reasons why *this* will be the year of the comeback.

Yet though the Chicago Cubs have made the playoffs a number of times in the past 15 years, it has been 103 years now since my team has won the World Series.

Does this discourage me? Of course! However, I optimistically remember that the Boston Red Sox won the World Series in 1918 and not again until 2004, 86 years later (and again in 2007!). If the Red Sox can do it, so can the Cubs. That's optimism, and I value it.

❖ Curious

I left Vanderbilt with a degree in—get ready—East Asian history and economics. Majors like this aren't chosen for the plentiful career options they offer. You choose them, especially if you grew up in a small, rural town in Indiana and your parents taught theology and Latin, because you are unrelentingly curious. And I am.

I believe intellectual curiosity leads to understanding that can drive positive change. So, expect me to ask a lot of questions.

❖ Mischievous

My sense of humor and mischievousness are a core part of my brand. I've found this trait useful in conversations with administrative assistants, CEOs, and plenty in between. Playfulness makes life and work more fun. However, it's been equally useful to ease tension when tempers flare.

❖ Impatient

I grew up in a town with one stoplight. In that rural Indiana burg, a long line consisted of three people; in other words, there wasn't much waiting. Now, when I go out to eat in the Kansas City suburb where I live, if the restaurant I've chosen has a wait of more than ten minutes, I get back in the car and find another.

This is not necessarily a strength, or even a good quality. But it is so much a part of me I'm not being fair if I don't include it in my brand.

So, these are my seven brand attributes. Yours will be different, but I trust they'll represent both the aspects of yourself that you're proud of, and some you'd rather not own, but are real for you.

Going public early on with your brand lets your people know something about who they're going to work with. And, with any luck, it offers them permission to let you get to know them, too. This is the starting place for any Get-Real Leadership team.

How "real" do you need to be?

In this brand-sharing exercise, do you fear being over-exposed? Do you feel pressure to disclose it all, but wonder about the wisdom? I don't know a definitive answer, but my own choice may be instructive.

My family is the soul of who I am. To say these people are important to me is like saying water is important to a fish. Does it surprise you that "Family-Oriented" did not show up as part of my personal brand? At first it surprised me. But then I realized my brand—and the Get-Real Leadership it empowers—isn't meant to fill every time and space in my life. It isn't a one-size-fits-all tool for opening myself to others. Because my family's importance simply can't be equal to "Mischievous" or "Optimistic" or "Tenacious," I intuitively concluded I'd be misrepresenting my family's significance if I simply made them one of seven logos in my life.

However, I have discovered through the years that the very fact of their absence provoked some interesting conversations with those I led, with equally interesting results.

Several years ago, when my two older kids were in elementary school (back when they still thought I was cool), I frequently joined them for lunch. I was very fortunate that their school was only two miles away from my office.

During one particular All-Hands Meeting when I was fairly new to my role, I had a question about my policy on work/life balance. "How many hours a week do you work?" the employee wanted to know.

In a move that was very atypical for me, I told them I wasn't going to answer the work-hours question. (As you'll see, I'm adamant about honesty with employees, so to refuse to answer a question caught the listeners off-guard.)

"This one," I said, "is something you have to answer for yourselves. You don't need to be working more or fewer hours than me; you need to do what's right for you with regards to your job and your family."

I realized immediately that though what I'd said was accurate, I wasn't really telling the whole story. Because we had a shared history as a team, this seemed like the right time to disclose more for their benefit.

"Years ago," I explained, "I decided to have lunch once a month with my elementary school kids. This mattered hugely to them and from their view seemed to be a genuine way to show I cared. So I started leaving the office once a month to do this.

"Occasionally I'd get a business call during one of these lunch times, and the caller might ask about all the background noise. 'I'm having corn dogs with 94 fourth graders,' I'd say, without apology or cover-up. 'Would you like me to step outside the lunch room so we can talk?'

"Most often, they'd laugh and encourage me to finish lunch, then call them back.

"My family is so much more important to me than my job that I don't even put them on the same plane," I explained. "And I'm so glad I didn't miss that opportunity with my kids. By middle school, having Dad at lunch wasn't cool anymore."

When I left that job a couple of years later, a dozen people wrote me or told me that this dialogue during the question and answer portion of an All-Hands Meeting changed their relationship with their job and their family. More than my words, it was my on-going actions that gave my folks permission to make work/life balance decisions without worrying about what the boss would think.

One said, "You gave me my family back. I now cook breakfast for my kids before school or drive them to school. These simple pleasures in life I had overlooked. You showed me how to balance my personal life and professional life."

I believe that this impact took place not in spite of the fact that "family" isn't on my brand statement, but because of it. I held back, if you will, part of me that matters very deeply, so that when the time and relationship could honor this level of sharing, I could offer it appropriately. The results were powerful.

So, when you've discovered what's real about you, find enjoyable, engaging ways to share it with those who need to know.

By doing this, you'll find you've opened a way for others to be more real with themselves and you, too. I have found that this mutual sharing leads to deeper relationships with the folks I work closely with and better business results.

4

Use Your Brand

- Keep yourself honest and accountable
- Make more consistent daily decisions
- Make better hires

Use your brand to keep yourself accountable

Knowing and sharing your brand is a great way to create personal accountability. After all, if I publicly declare who I am and what matters to me, won't people expect me to live up to it? (It's a little like going public with the commitment that you're going to lose twenty pounds by Christmas.)

I've found the potential embarrassment and incongruity of not being consistent has motivated me to make better choices when the stakes were high.

With a commitment to authenticity, we don't hide from knowing there's a gap. We want to know. I want to know. Periodically, I ask myself, "If my current team didn't know my seven words, how would they describe my brand?"

It is important to occasionally recheck your seven words/personal brand via 360 degree feedback (given anonymously, of course!) I do this every year or two so I don't lose touch with who I am vs. who I want to be.

Use your brand to make better decisions

We're going to talk a little baseball, so non-sports fans, stay with me. Though we'll start with a tutorial about win/loss ratios, we'll end in a place you'll find useful in making the small—and big—decisions every day. For me, baseball is the easiest way to make an enormously important point about the power of realness and the impact it can have cumulatively on success.

Ready?

There are 162 games in a baseball season. Every team in the major leagues is going to lose 40 and win 40 no matter how good it is and no matter how large or small of a payroll it carries. The fact is no team is perfectly bad or perfectly good. However, there are 82 *other* games that each team plays in a season.

You know what happens in those other 82? While size of payroll may be a factor, history has proven (Tampa Bay Rays, Florida Marlins, Minnesota Twins, etc.) that no matter whether you spend a lot or a little on players, the winning teams do all the little things extremely well.

They hit the cut-off man in the fifth inning, make the right pitching change at the right time, turn the double play in a crucial situation, advance the runners when appropriate, block the ball in the dirt with a runner on third and they win frequently—often by one or two runs. They win 62 and lose only 20 of those other 82 games.

In total, they win 102 games and go to the World Series. These teams wind up with parades, adulation, higher-paid players. Life is good. The cumulative effect of dozens of little, positive and productive choices, decisions, and plays enables them to tip the balance and win a majority of the games that are toss-ups. These teams find a way to win at the margin when the game is in the balance.

The not-so-good teams have the opposite experience. They don't do the little things well. These teams make a bad pitching change, fail to turn the double-play, miss the cut-off man in a crucial situation, and drop a difficult pop up. They win only 20 and lose 62 of these "close call" games, for a total of 60 wins and 102 losses.

They wind up firing the manager, demoting players, and whining about low attendance.

The difference in the results of winning and losing can be enormous. *However, the actions and choices that bring us to the win or the loss are often incredibly small and, at the time, seemingly insignificant.*

We can underplay the importance of daily attitudes and decisions because they don't seem important enough to move the world. However, it's the cumulative effect of all these small, daily choices that over time determine who we are and what our lives become.

Being clear about your brand can increase the possibility that you'll be more consistent as you make dozens or perhaps hundreds of decisions that make up daily life.

You've established to yourself and others what's authentically true for you. That work doesn't have to be revisited with every decision.

You've freed yourself to simply use your brand to make consistent, authentic decisions that over time will help you live true to yourself.

In the end, actions speak louder than words. With a clearly established sense of yourself, your chances of acting consistently will increase.

You'll find this much more effective than if you focused on some cheesy promotional campaign to "communicate your credibility."

You want to be real with yourself, and to live real. Clarifying your brand will help you do that in hundreds of small decisions every day. Through the cumulative effect of these many, small choices, Get-Real Leadership will emerge for you.

Use branding to generate better hires

Hiring the right people is so critical—and so tough—that teaching good ways to do it ought to take up a whole semester in MBA programs.

As I began to lead teams, I soon learned that resumes weren't to be trusted as a real picture of how the candidate might perform.

Think about it. The system is far too close to dating. They're on their best behavior; you are on yours. The back-and-forth dance sets you both up to emphasize the best about your side of the equation.

(Do you believe we've ever really heard an honest answer to the question, "Tell me about your weaknesses"? Or ever *given* an honest answer?)

Fairly early in the game I decided to look first at internal candidates when I had openings. And I decided to use the "personal branding" approach to get a more realistic take on who would be a good fit.

When I came to serious consideration of a candidate, I nosed around until I found people in the company who knew the candidate well. Then I'd wait until 8:00 p.m. or so, and call these people on their work phone so I'd be sure to get voicemail.

I told them I was considering such-and-such employee for a place on my team. It would help me get a better picture if they'd leave a voicemail for me with seven words they felt best described the person. I'd reiterate I didn't want a call back, just a voicemail. I wasn't interested in a conversation about the person or a traditional reference. Actually, it was the gut-response, non-traditional information I was seeking.

Also, I made it clear I didn't need sentences or explanations—just seven stand-alone words to give me a picture of the person.

As you probably guessed, few people gave clearly negative descriptors.

However, by putting together the feedback of several people who worked with my candidate, it was surprisingly easy to create a picture that usually proved to be accurate. For example, I really want "teamwork" and "positive attitude" to be a part of a person's brand if they are going to be on my team. The absence of these is a warning.

The branding process is a simple and useful feedback mechanism that can make your organization stronger in multiple ways.

Once you've established what "real" looks like for you, you can begin to apply these truths to the way you manage people and your business. We'll explore both in the chapters ahead.

"The answer to three questions will determine your success or failure:

Can people trust me to do my best?
Am I committed to the task in hand?
Do I care about other people and show it?

If the answers to all three questions are yes, there is no way you can fail."

— **Lou Holtz**

5

Connect

- Make optimism your lead card
- Set team members up for success

Hire for positive attitude

As I was moving up in the business world I believed hiring top-notch talent was the deal-breaker for success. If the attitude of the folks you found was good, that was a nice bonus, but it wasn't nearly as important as the talent they possessed.

Over the past fifteen years, I've made a 180-degree turn. I still believe that there's a talent bar that must be cleared. However, that bar is a lot lower than I would have ever thought when I first began my business career.

I realize there are many, many talented people with the ability to do most any job I have to offer. What is much more scarce, and therefore more valuable, is a great attitude.

With reasonable talent and a great attitude, the sky is the limit. Give me someone who says, "We're going to battle until we succeed, obstacles or no. We'll figure out how to make the impossible happen, and we are going to win."

Optimism created the "98/2 Rule"

The employee policies in too many organizations assume that left to their own devices, employees are going to do bad things. Leaders feel the need to set up rules against every conceivable bad behavior and pay someone to monitor the employees so these behaviors don't slip past them.

Instead, I think about employees with my own 98/2 rule. Unless we've been complete idiots in our hiring processes, 98 percent of our employees want to do well. They come to work with a desire to produce and make the work experience a good one for them, for the others around them, and for the company.

That means maybe 2 percent don't look and act like this. For this 2 percent, we need enough clear expectations and consequences to quickly identify them and help them either change or find another place to work.

To do otherwise isn't fair to the 98 percent and will only discourage these productive associates.

Ah, but with the 98 percent, leaders need to focus their time and energy listening to them and working hard to make the place they work and the ways they work wonderful. If you can do this, the sky is the limit.

Let trust shape your policy decisions

When sales or service take place in a call center setting, it really matters that the phones are staffed when we tell customers they're going to be. Without this expectation in place, callers wind up in those damnable queues that make for such humiliating (to us) and funny (to everyone else) YouTube videos of the poor slob stuck in elevator-music land while the seasons change around him.

This scheduling challenge, paired with the assumption that call centers hire transients who are there to earn a few bucks until they can do something better, lead to some interesting policies.

For example, when I first began one of my roles, I learned our call centers had a policy called the "Five-Minute Rule." If employees clocked in more than five minutes after the agreed-upon start time, they were given what we called an "occurrence." Three occurrences resulted in a "tardy," and three tardies meant you'd be fired.

This "three-strikes-you're-out!" approach had downsides, from my view. The call center would be left with a turn-over and hiring process to fill the empty chair that cost close to $13,000 when we factored in recruiting, training, and lost productivity.

Looking at this problem from a Get-Real perspective suggested a different way of thinking. Maybe, instead of sitting at home every day plotting how to come in late and shave time off their workday, most employees wanted to produce at their jobs. But maybe, just like for all the rest of us, life intervened in inconvenient ways. Traffic. Road construction. Sick children. Day care issues.

What would happen if we assumed our call center reps were motivated and well-meaning people who needed rules generated from an assumption of trust, rather than an assumption of abuse?

From this thinking, my call center managers came up with a proposal. We replaced the Five-Minute Rule with a new, more flexible expectation. They called it "Give 'Em Eight."

In other words, employees were paid for an eight-hour day, and they were expected to work eight. But they had a 60-minute window in which they could start the eight hours, with the understanding they'd adjust their leave time accordingly.

The outcome was amazing. As you might expect, employee engagement scores went up in the call centers and employee turnover decreased dramatically, decreasing expenditures for recruiting and training new employees.

What about . . . ?

People who hear me tell this story push back immediately with one question: how did you make sure the phones were covered if you couldn't count on people showing up at a prescribed time? I wondered about this myself. It was a risk we acknowledged, but decided to take for the sake of employee engagement.

As it turned out, employees' arrival times didn't tend to vary much from the schedules they had established before we offered the "Give 'Em Eight" policy. They'd generally arranged their lives to fit a schedule, and apparently it worked better for them to keep that schedule.

What *did* change was their anxiety. Under the new plan, if there was a traffic backup on the way to work, or a babysitter snafu, they didn't have to worry about a black mark on their record.

The focus now became getting the job done in a reasonable, respectful way, and they responded with reason and respect in return.

There were abuses, of course, from employees who came in late and *also* left early. But this system was so helpful to the vast majority of motivated employees, it became self-monitoring. The employees would pay attention to and reprimand the abusers. They'd say, "This system is great for us. You think it's great for you because you start late and leave early, and no one calls you on it. But it's not okay with us. Give your eight, just like we do, and *don't* mess it up for all the rest of us!"

When you expect the best and listen to your people when they tell you how they can give more, you win and they do, too.

Care enough to get them in the right place

When my wife Kris became a supervisor in an insurance claims division, she was asked to begin administrative action against an employee on her team who was not making the weekly quota.

Kris was 23 years old at the time; her employee had been with the company for 25 years and was raising her grandchild. The simplest and lowest-risk answer for a young manager would have been to document the poor performance and send the employee out the door.

Instead, Kris researched the employee's history and found she'd received consistently positive feedback while at her past position in the department's accounting group. Clearly, this wasn't an underachiever. Maybe the issue was one of fit.

Kris talked to the accounting supervisor and discovered there was an open position. Because of the employee's past record, the department was willing and even happy to take her back. So, instead of facing unemployment, this employee got to move back to a place of success.

This kind of managerial commitment to our people is crucial to Get-Real Leadership.

Otherwise, we can be like the football coach whose team is seven points behind and invests his time yelling from the sidelines, "Hey! We're behind! Can't you see we are behind? Just two more minutes to quit being behind!

"And being behind means we're going to lose, which makes us losers. Do you want that?"

In this setting, I'd be like the quarterback who comes over and says, "Coach, we're actually aware we are behind. This is not news to us. Just like you, we don't want to lose. So, how about putting your energy into helping us figure out how we can win?"

Set reasonable targets

One of my bosses and I argued over the whole idea of performance goals. He contended that "you've got to set your targets out of reach, knowing full well they're out of reach. Trying to reach something very, very high, even if you miss it, will create better production than if you aim lower."

I disagree.

I believe if both my people and I know we can't reach the goals we've set, we lose. Score: Arrogance, 1 and Get Real, 0. I do believe in stretch goals—that's a passion for competition I'll talk more about in the next section. But I try to never set goals that are more than 50 percent beyond what I think we could realistically reach.

These goals push us and bring out the best in us. Because I believe we do have a chance of meeting them, I'm wholehearted and honest when I inspire, motivate, push, and pull my people to do so. When we achieve them, we celebrate together—we then move on with energy to a new set of goals.

We need to give our people a reasonable chance of winning. Anything else is less than real.

Reward attitude, not just production

After success with Walmart, I came back to P&G headquarters thinking of myself as the Big Man on Campus.

I knew from my bosses that a promotion lay ahead, and I imagined myself responsible for one of the high-profile, deal-breaker brands. I did get assigned one of the highly visible brands. This one was a $100+ million business, with millions in profits yearly. That's a money producer capable of getting any 30-year-old excited about leading it.

Unfortunately, the big-ass brand to which I was assigned turned out to be Metamucil. Constipation as a calling? Not exactly how I'd envisioned my career trajectory in grad school.

When I met the leadership team I'd inherited, I found they were sheepish to be working on this brand. They were tired of being the butt of everyone's jokes (sorry, had to say it!), and this sense of embarrassment sloshed over to their own teams.

Though a positive attitude is in my DNA, it didn't take me long to see where they were coming from.

You haven't lived until you've spent four hours behind a one-way mirror listening to a room full of middle-aged women talk about their elimination issues. Then you had to care enough to provide thoughtful follow-up questions to the focus group moderator.

I realized then I'd signed on for a potentially lucrative, but socially awkward assignment.

If I didn't help my team get over this awkwardness, we'd never be able to win at the level this product—and these people—deserved.

I figured I could spend a lot of money on improve-your-self-esteem speakers, or just tackle the issue head on. The next time the team met, we announced the formation of an award, to be presented each month when the team got together. It wasn't an award for production, I told them, but rather for having a great attitude.

"To nominate someone," I explained, "just think of the person in our business you'd most like to walk down the hall with. No matter what their job is, they make every day a good one, and you know your day is going to be better because you ran into them. It's the opposite of the person you email with questions, even though they sit in the next cube, because you just can't stand to be with them."

I made it clear all nominations would come straight to me since I'd be the Committee of One making the selection.

Of course I knew that having all nominations come to me would get the attention of these competitive up-and-comers. When the new boss creates an initiative, it's to your advantage to get on board quickly.

Now they were ready to hear more.

"The name of this recognition is . . ." I paused for effect ". . . the Mr. Happy Bowel Award!"

I then whipped out an intestine-colored tee shirt with a cartoon sketch of Mr. Happy Bowel, a strange-looking guy in a top hat whose body was basically one big intestine, and who grinned ear-to-ear as he waved a canister of Metamucil in each hand. The slogan above him trumpeted, "With Friends Like These Who Needs Enemas?" The back of the tee shirt was going to say: "It's Hard to Be #1 in the #2 Business." However, we dropped that idea. (Yeah, yeah, I know . . . really bad. But no one remembers to give credit for the slogans we decided *not* to use, and there were some pretty disgusting ones, I can assure you.)

There was a moment of silence, then someone groaned, and another started to laugh. For whatever we were going to become together, the expectation had now been set that we were going to *own* this brand, even if it meant making fun of ourselves. Those who owned it publicly were going to be those with the best, most positive attitudes—the people others most wanted to be like.

I didn't know if the idea would take hold, but the second month we gave the award, the first winner wore his (ugly) new shirt to the team meeting.

At the month three presentation, winners one and two both showed up sporting Mr. Happy Bowel on their chests. By month seven, the word was out across the company, and the shirts became a major badge of honor.

Marketing gurus would tell you that getting the "opinion leaders" in any organization to champion an unpopular message is going to move acceptance along much faster. But honestly, I was 30 at the time and didn't think that deeply. I was a leader trying to run a successful business, and though I didn't know much, I knew that if we weren't genuinely positive about the business we were in, no amount of internal PR would overcome it.

My learning from the runaway success of the "Mr. Happy Bowel Award" was this: if you expect the best from employees and praise them when they're giving what you expect, you'll get more of it.

So later, when I moved to Sprint, the "Mr. Happy Bowel" idea stayed with me. I did consider keeping the "Happy Bowel" theme since the Sprint long-distance products ran on fiber optics, and Metamucil was also about fiber, but I rightly guessed few would get the joke.

I shifted the title to the "Hoosier Hysteria Award," in honor of my home state and the great team spirit exhibited by the Hoosiers, who don't put players' names on the back of their jerseys to create team focus. I also added the restriction that when you nominated someone, there could be no copying anyone on the email, or your nomination would be thrown out. (This kept the attention-seekers who nominated their bosses, etc., from getting airtime.)

I also reserved the right to give out no awards (this happened a couple of times) or multiple awards (once I gave out seven at one time) to make the point that it was attitude I was after, not delivering against a quota or maintaining some artificial awards system.

I did make a significant change that recipients appreciated. I began numbering the "Hoosier Hysteria" shirts. I have now given out 196 of these in the past fifteen years and those wearing them are a part of a fairly exclusive club as a result of their positive attitudes. Once again, those t-shirts were coveted because of what they stood for.

When we ask people to follow us, we're asking for their trust that we'll do right by them. Using a leadership platform to proclaim and demonstrate positivity toward them is one of the quickest and most lasting ways to a Get-Real Leadership connection.

6

Communicate

- Talk honestly
- Help team members speak openly to you

Don't use fifty words if one will do

I helped run an All-Hands Meeting that was important enough to pull in four other senior executives besides myself. We'd each taken our turn at energizing the hotel ballroom packed with employees. Now the Q&A time had come round, so we took our seats on the stools on the stage and waited for questions from employees.

As they came, the answers got longer, bigger, and, well, smarter. Each "what are we going to do about . . . " query seemed to produce a more complex, more business-buzzword-crammed answer.

Rationales, caveats, options, back-up strategies; it was all there. It was as if we were part of a secret competition to see who could pack the most syllables into an answer.

Then a question was directed to me. At that moment, "Get-Real Harry" trumped "Show 'em your MBA Harry" and I stopped, looked straight at the questioner, and answered with just one word: "No." Just no, the direct answer to a direct question.

Silence followed. Then the crowd broke into spontaneous cheers and applause.

They weren't cheering for smart or smart-ass. They were cheering real.

To this day, I don't remember the question. But I'll never forget the power of cutting through over-complicated rhetoric and simply giving a real answer that anyone can get.

Put corporate-speak in its place

I've gotten tired enough of communication-killing corporate speak that I now sometimes start presentations to new groups of employees with this introduction.

"Hello. I'm Harry Campbell, and I'd like to share with you my leadership vision."

Cue PowerPoint slide in Ariel Bold that says this:

> "My vision is to always strive to dramatically improve my customer-centric view of the business landscape. I relentlessly drive myself and the teams I manage, to leverage synergies, integrate productized services, and monetize our human capital."
>
> "My mission is to optimize customer touch points, facilitate inter-disciplinary technologies, shift current paradigms, and be globally recognized as best-in-class, the benchmark in our sandbox."

Pause. Then I slap up a slide that says: "THAT'S NOT REAL!!" I then show a slide of a giant bingo card with one buzzword in each box. They laugh as I point out I'd have gotten Bingo diagonally if I'd added the word "innovation" to my leadership mission!

Get-Real Leadership has to be founded on the simple beauty of honest, direct communication.

Stop dancing around the real issues

I know you've heard it.

An employee asks, "Why don't we open a retail store in Sometown?" The MBA-worthy and Corporate-Counsel-Approved Answer goes like this:

"Our previous study of the macroeconomic factors of the Sometown region indicates sub-par potential for profitability of a new power of presence in the retail channel. We will continue to utilize and leverage relevant data to determine a point for which a paradigm shift in our current strategy is appropriate."

When we use corporate speak like this, we lose the chance for real relationships built on trust with our employees. Plus, they come up with their own versions of the truth when they can see we are dancing around directness. The real answer here should have been this: "We have not been able to make money with a retail store in towns with less than 15,000 people. For now, we will continue to build stores in towns with a population greater than 15,000."

There is a path that involves speaking to your people the way you want to be spoken to. You want the truth, and you want it in language that makes sense. Right?

I'm not dismissing the pressure on us when we've been told by higher-ups there are answers we can and cannot give. Get-Real Leadership doesn't mean blabbing out everything you know and every guess you feel inclined to make to every employee you meet. But communication that builds trust tells everything you can in language anyone can understand. When there are answers you can't give, you still speak directly.

A few years ago, when the company for which I worked was being purchased by another, employees were rightfully fearful about their futures in the new company. So, "water cooler talk" centered for weeks on two words used by the CEO when asked about people keeping their jobs.

Since the acquiring company would be making the go-forward decisions, and workforce decisions were months away, the CEO had been coached to say that even though concrete numbers weren't available, the company would maintain a "significant presence" in the city where the current headquarters was located.

Significant presence? What the hell did that mean? Significant compared with what? Interpretations and rumors ran rampant. Everyone made best guesses. But my prize for the best interpretation went to the front-line employee who declared to co-workers, "I know exactly what a 'significant presence' means—it means I get to keep *my* job. Now, that's *significant!*"

The point is, employees recognize bluffing. I believe they can live with uncertainty better than a bluff. "I don't know" is an answer. And if it is accompanied with "here are some of the factors that will determine the answer" or "here's what we're doing to find out the answer" or "here's an idea of when we'll know more about the answer," you've respected Get-Real Leadership.

Speaking to the "hidden question" can make a difference, too. In this example, were the employees concerned about how many of them would be retained or what would happen to them if they were let go? I'd venture it's the latter. In this situation, going after the facts and helping people prepare in case the news isn't good can show respect and grace—it makes up for what either you don't know or can't say.

Bottom line: truth is respectful; evasiveness isn't.

It's not communication if you're the only one talking. . .

If two-way dialogue isn't involved, you may call it an announcement or information sharing, but don't call it communication.

Because you carry both the privilege and the responsibility for how the workplace will be structured, you need to send Get-Real messages and provide simple ways for employees to provide Get-Real messages to you. Any other approach is a dead-end.

Our people aren't stupid. They know the income they bring home to their families is dependent on our choice to continue to employ them.

So, unless I put protections in place, smart employees will laugh at my jokes, funny or not, and be careful to tell me what I want to hear (best case) or not tell me what I don't want to hear (worst case).

It's not enough to make some blanket announcement about your "open door policy." In reality, the intimidation inherent in walking into your boss's office to ask a tough question or deliver tough feedback is show-stopping for nearly all but the boldest—or dumbest—of us. Human resources professionals have told me they even have trouble getting honest answers from departing employees about why they're leaving the company. "Don't burn bridges" is the advice guiding many of them.

Show them you listened

So how are you going to find out what they think about what's working and what isn't? I've tried a number of approaches. Here are some that worked better than others.

I invited 15-20 employees at a time to sign up for hour-long feedback sessions with my lead team and me. Our commitment for these sessions was this: any question was fine, and—if at all possible—the employee would have an answer to his or her question before the phone call ended.

We scheduled these "answer sessions" weekly, and after a staff meeting, my team would head to the phones to talk with employees. Sometimes my team knew the answers. If they didn't, they'd put the conference call on hold and head over to the area responsible for getting the answer or even bring the subject matter expert onto the call right then.

As you can imagine, the impact of these call-in Q&A chats went well beyond the employees who participated. Reports about their experiences traveled like lightening across the businesses where they worked. So, besides giving us the chance to get real information to employees, we got the additional lift of employees understanding that we'd kept our one-to-one, real-time answers promise.

Another benefit was we were able to keep our finger on the pulse of the business. We knew what was on our employees' minds because we were providing a simple, non-threatening forum for them to ask us questions.

In a world built on public relations spin, the power of one-to-one, voice-to-voice interaction between employee and boss can pay huge dividends.

When employees call the boss

I also instituted a policy that anyone in my business could call or email me directly about anything *without* having to copy their boss on the email.

If you work in a large company, does this sound scary or even ridiculous? Do you imagine hundreds of emails flooding your already over-filled inbox every day? Or prestige-seeking employees taking up your time in an attempt to impress? Or whiny, tattletale employees overdosing on complaints about their unsuspecting managers?

That isn't how it worked. In reality, even when I had thousands of associates in my organization and I repeatedly let them know they could communicate directly with me, I received only two or three emails a week. The cool thing is the messages were most often focused on improving the business, such as a new product idea or a new market to target. Occasionally they were complaints about a leader who the reporting employee didn't like.

When I got people-related complaints, I'd assure the employee I'd check it out, and ask if they'd allow me to use their name (some did; most didn't).

I made good on my word by calling the leader of the group in question to report there had been questions raised and ask for their input. The responses were varied. Sometimes the manager in question was struggling and needed either more coaching and help or a move elsewhere. Their leader knew this, and the employee complaint simply helped move along a decision that was pending anyway.

Other times, the manager would be one of our very strong performers, but it was known already that there was an unhappy team member who had self-identified and needed an intervention. HR was a big help in these moments.

Interestingly, when the complainant needed a shift in attitude or role, and we provided opportunity for one or both, we found the general impact very moralizing to the team. Instead of the message being, "Complain to Harry about your manager and you'll wind up getting canned," it became "Complaints get handled fairly for both employees and managers, and the teams will function better *no matter how* the complaints are handled."

Time waster?

The main concern from my staff when I inaugurated this "feel free to call Harry" program was that my time would be wasted. They shouldn't have worried.

Only once do I recall what most people would have said was a totally silly message. A call-center rep emailed me to complain that the phone rep sitting next to her chewed his gum too loudly. Would I please make him stop?

When my team heard about this, the leader who managed this call center was embarrassed, and others talked about how to set better rules for the process so my time wasn't wasted.

I saw it completely differently. I was the one who had personally opened the invitation for direct communication; shutting down the employee didn't make sense to me.

Instead, I saw this as a great teaching opportunity for my managers on how to respond to employee issues. So I did what I'd expect them to do: I checked first with HR to see what our company policy was on the gum-chewing question. If this had been against policy, I'd want to be sure I understood where the policy originated and might even ask whether or not it made sense, but that didn't prove to be necessary.

As it turned out, when reps weren't on the phone with customers, our policies said they could chew all the gum they wanted. Now, general behavior that created havoc in the call center would have been prohibited under other, very reasonable policies. But behaving in ways that simply annoyed the owner of the cube next door wasn't something we wrote policies against. (Really, aren't some things just common sense?)

So, I wrote a response to the call center rep, telling her the policy and why this particular behavior wasn't prohibited. I then suggested that either ear plugs or ear phones might be useful between calls.

She wrote back and thanked me.

I made good on my Get-Real communication commitment by listening and responding respectfully to a front-line employee, and my team got a chance to think through and help their managers think through how they dealt with employee complaints that seemed superfluous to them. We'd have missed all this without the open communication policy.

One consideration

I will add a caveat, however.

When you try this approach, if you find your email fills up daily with 40-50 messages that look to you like whiney complaints or ridiculous ideas that have little relevance to the business, then you've given yourself a wonderful diagnostic tool.

You can then ask, "What do my people think about positivity? Or about ownership? Or accountability?" Or you can ask, "How much do my people know about our business realities and how they work?"

In the next section of the book, we're going to talk about Get-Real Leadership in your business, and we'll work more on how to build a competitive workplace that focuses on the positive.

But for now, these unfiltered messages from employees—if most of them are downers for you—can be a cheap, very direct source of feedback to point you clearly toward changes that need to be made.

I'm not saying they show the need for changes in who you've hired. I'm championing changes first in how you define and communicate expectations for your people and how you and your team model what you want a great workplace to be.

Getting feedback may require investments

Once my employee numbers got past 2,500, I realized I'd have to work even harder to hear them. So I created a mini-function with a couple of excellent people with marketing skills and an employee engagement passion and asked them to create ways to keep the communication flowing.

They created internal surveys, followed by focus groups that worked just like the surveys we used for customers. Because the employees they spoke with didn't report directly to them, and they were given free reign to promise anonymity, they pulled in great stuff that kept my team immeasurably closer to our employees' reality.

I still had my open email policy during this time, but with such a large organization I needed additional tools to collect real feedback.

Creating honest, two-way communication is a total win. There isn't a downside, if you're willing to be real with your people and allow them to be real with you.

7

Cover Their Butts

- Cover for your team with upper management
- Cover for them when they are most vulnerable

Keep your boss out of their hair

Some of the most useful work we do for our employees involves keeping our boss out of their way so they can get on with the work that produces results.

I am not talking about smarmy, underhanded cover-ups to hide behaviors that embarrass us from our bosses. Rather, I'm advocating we manage unreasonable expectations made by our leaders that we know don't really contribute to success and keep our people busy but not productive.

For instance, one senior executive I worked for felt he needed to be involved in marketing—down to approving the wording on our print ads.

Hell, I didn't even get that involved; I expected the advertising people we had hired to design and produce great campaigns. But for whatever reason, this particular aspect of what we did to drive revenue and profits held great interest for our leader.

I could have had my advertising team run the "almost final" work by me so we could together run everything by my boss. But in doing this, I would have been assigning a bunch of highly paid professionals the role of flunkies who waited for marching orders, then carried them out line by line. These talented employees deserved a better chance to contribute than that.

So, I stepped back and looked at the situation from my boss's point of view. He had more to do, of course, than tweak words on a print ad—I knew it, and he knew it. Maybe a more appropriate and meaningful role for him would be in the setting of our strategic direction, much earlier in the process than after the print ads were developed.

So instead of bringing him completed campaigns for his approval, we moved his input back to the strategic stage of the process.

As we decided on general approaches suggested by our testing, business results, and marketing information, we developed several viable options—and he gave good input early on to the direction we'd chosen.

With this shift, by the time the work got as granular as the design of the print ads, he was already familiar with the direction and had some ownership because he'd been a decision maker with regards to the strategy. The advertising people got much more freedom with the elimination of do-overs, and the senior executive had more confidence and pride in the direction of our advertising. A win for all.

On most everything else, I made sure I spent plenty of time with my boss, informing, answering questions, and getting input, so the team responsible for the work didn't have to. They needed marching orders they could depend on, rather than ones that shifted as a result of meetings (late in the process) with my boss.

Managing up like this takes varying amounts of time, depending on the boss. When you choose to do it, you're doing for your people what they can't do for themselves.

Take bold steps when expectations aren't realistic
One of the leaders I worked for had a reputation as a "prove-it-to-me" stickler for detail.

The word on the street was this: for Monday morning staff meetings, you'd better have detailed information and answers to explain the results from the previous week. In addition, you'd better come with back-up hand-outs or presentations in case the discussion required more detail.

As a result, on Sunday afternoons and evenings a huge number of our folks were in the office. Their role was to provide me with all the information I might need in the Monday morning staff meeting. Please understand, I was asked to give a short verbal update on the results from the previous week and my team was putting dozens of hours into preparing me. The thought was that I needed to be ready for virtually any question.

This made no sense to me. First of all, the employees had lives and kids and obligations. Plus, if our people were going to give up their valuable time on a weekend, I wanted to be sure it was an emergency situation that would make a difference in our profitability (put your team's energy to use vs. the outside world) —not in our impression on my boss.

I also wondered how my team saw the man I worked for. Was he for us or against us? What did he want from these staff meeting updates? Was it an academic exercise to see which of us could retain or bring more minutiae about the business? Or did he want to know we were producing results against the profitability goals?

I decided to take the latter interpretation.

Instead of preparing myself for a detailed presentation and discussion, I kept it simple and reported the highlights for the past week and touched on key issues we were facing in the near term. I handled questions as effectively as possible and was not concerned if my real answer was that I didn't know, but I'd let them know.

I never heard a negative word from him about these updates. Better yet, my people had weekends to spend as they wished versus grinding away in the office preparing me for a brief verbal update in a staff meeting. I came to this approach by deciding to start simple and take a chance on my boss's reasonableness. Had he reacted to the first discussion with a reprimand and requirement for more data or detail, and a conversation between us didn't result in my understanding the need for this, I might have had to rethink my approach or even ask myself whether or not we should be working together.

That didn't happen. But my people needed me to take a chance on their behalf—put myself on the line first—to save them from work I didn't see as productive.

Show well on their behalf

The mischievous part of me likes to surprise and appear a bubble or two off-center.

However, the times I don't indulge this very real part of me are when I'm representing the company in public forums.

For example, when I worked at Embarq I was responsible for over 40 percent of the revenue we generated. Since Embarq was publicly held, we needed to talk with investors and financial analysts on a quarterly basis about our results. We were there to explain the results and show the company's strengths; the analysts were there to learn as much as possible, find the holes, and try to pry more information from us than we intended to disclose.

When I spoke on the company's behalf in these sessions, the analysts got the suit-and-tie, stay-on-script version of me. Serving my people—and the CEO and shareholders—meant this was no time to show off, grandstand, or speak lightly. I respected how much was at stake in these meetings, and though I would sometimes joke a little, I was very careful to be sure that when we left the meeting, the CEO would say, "Thanks. You represented us skillfully, and there were no surprises."

Get-Real Leadership is my guiding principle. It's not just about connecting to my team members in ways that are genuine; it's about understanding I represent them to others when I present us in public venues. I want to show well so they show well. They deserve no less.

Protect them from looking stupid to customers

Telecom is what business types call a "mature" industry. Nearly everyone has a telephone. Therefore, fresh profitability isn't going to come from selling to large pockets of people who have neither a landline phone nor a cell phone. In industries like this, new customers are to be found by wooing them away from the competition.

This is the reason behind those better-than-believable offers from communications companies you find every other day in your mailbox and on television ads. It's a standard game in our world to come up with an amazingly low sign-up offer that will interest and attract people who are paying more to one of our competitors so we can get them to sign a contract with us.

We undercut our own profitability—introduce "loss leaders," if you will—in the hope that people who sign with us will stay.

All well and good. Unless you're the sales rep in one of our call centers or retail stores who has to explain to a 23-year customer of our company that she is not eligible for the greatly reduced rates on the product she buys from us because these deals are reserved for new customers only.

Think about it. A customer has stayed with you faithfully for 23 years, contributing month after month to a positive bottom line. Now when there's a perk to be had, it goes not to the faithful partner but to someone who has done nothing for the company to date.

It didn't take long for me to realize what an untenable position I was putting my employees in when I asked them to defend this proposition to customers.

So, we stopped doing it. Any deal we gave to new customers we also gave—enthusiastically—to existing customers who wanted it. Simple as that.

Of course, you can imagine the pushback we got when we first introduced this decision. What about the financial losses (aka write-downs) from giving current customers lower rates? Some predicted these losses for one major offering could exceed $100 million. Before this specific proposal was approved, the modeling required by the finance group included an expectation that at least 20 percent of the "takers" for a new offer would be current customers converting to the lower rate.

As it turned out, total sales for this offer dramatically exceeded expectations and well under 10 percent of the sales were to current customers. In addition, the current customers that did take the new rate stayed with us longer (lower churn) and were much more satisfied customers.

In other words, the losses predicted by the finance group were much smaller than forecasted, while we gained big time from picking up new customers.

Later, when our company was sold and I explained this policy to one of the new leaders, he insisted it simply couldn't work for their customer base. So, I challenged him to check the numbers.

When his company issued one of these "great rates for new customers only" offers, how many existing customers called in to complain and eventually were given the lower rate too? He thought this did not happen. The data actually showed he was wrong. Existing customers would call in to get the lower rate, be told they weren't eligible and threaten to disconnect. They would be transferred to the "save desk" and, after considerable wrangling, be given the lower rate.

So, these loyal customers came away with the same lower price they would have started with under our system, but the company got a bad reputation from the way the discounting was handled and incurred higher customer service costs. What was the logic in that approach?

This principle of treating current customers as well or better than new customers generated huge increases in sales and profits, as well as lower churn. So it was clearly "right" for our customers.

It was also right and logical for our employees. They now had a principle they believed in and were able to easily explain and defend it to current, loyal customers as well as prospects. In the end, everyone won.

Protect them from their own immaturity

Talent does not always come in a mature package; sometimes it needs time and experience to grow into what it can be.

In these growing-up years it's possible to make some pretty embarrassing mistakes. You've seen them, and I've made them!

During one team meeting, we were struggling hard to decide about a tough business issue. Verbal wrestling went on and strong opinions came out, particularly from one of my most talented young leaders. When everyone had had his or her say it was clear there'd be no consensus, and I knew we had to move ahead. So, I made the decision.

The direction I chose, however, wasn't the one supported by my talented young VP.

She made her disapproval clear. "So, I guess that's how it's going to be," she muttered sarcastically and with a clearly audible sigh. And she turned away, dropped her eyes to her phone, and completely disengaged from the team. In fact, she began texting furiously.

I closed the meeting as if nothing untoward had happened, and we went on to our work. Later in a one-to-one, I talked very directly to the leader and let her know what her behavior seemed to say about teamwork. I didn't hold back. But publicly no one else was privy to our conversation. I didn't use it as a public teaching example or see a need to bring it up again with her.

I didn't believe I was seeing insurrection, just immaturity. In that moment she needed protection from herself, and a bad choice she'd likely not make again as she grew as a leader.

Leadership comes with a larger responsibility than what our people carry. However, it also offers larger opportunities to help employees be successful if we care enough to cover for them when they need it.

*"You must never confuse faith that you will prevail
—which you can never afford to lose—
with the discipline to confront
the most brutal facts of your current reality,
whatever they might be."*

— William Stockdale,
as quoted by Jim Collins in *Good to Great*

8

Step Up

- Own your stuff
- Excuses: don't make them; don't accept them

Is your work today about promotion or production?

Are you living in the life you have now, doing the job you have now? Or are you actually putting your interest and energy into imagining the job you want to have when you've been promoted out of this deadly-dull place in which you currently find yourself?

If so, s-t-o-p. Stop.

If you aren't giving 100 percent to the job you have at this place, if you aren't *owning* it, you won't at the next place, either.

If you aren't finding a way to thrive right here, right now, you won't thrive in the next place either.

If your eye is on the next prize, you will stumble over the prize that is right in front of you.

When I hear people in my organization tell me they're mad because of being overlooked for a promotion, I say, "Show me. Show me what you're doing where you are right now. Are you exceeding your goals? Are you markedly better at your current job than others who are doing the same work? Are you out-producing everyone else around you? If so, let's talk. If not, start over-producing, pull together the results, and *then* let's talk."

Own your stuff. You know what your stuff is. It's these co-workers, this job, this place, this time, this economy, this company, these customers, this boss. It's yours. Own it. Claim it. And make something of it, rather than spending your mental energy somewhere else, in some other company, with some other customers, selling some other business proposition from some other platform.

Pressure to avoid accountability is always lurking

I speak so clearly about this because I deeply understand the temptation to avoid ownership.

Several years ago I was speaking in an All-Hands Meeting of my organization, and delivered some news and policy decisions I didn't personally agree with. And when I did, I talked about what "they" had decided and "their" thinking about the situation.

When it came time for Q&A, one of the employees came back with an accountability challenge that hit me between the eyes. "Harry," he said, "you are one of the top leaders in this Fortune 500 company. Who exactly are 'they' to you?"

There are moments that allow for no glib answer, because the question is itself the answer. I was caught up short. I didn't look to the senior leadership of this organization; I *was* that senior leadership. I was part of the "they" who made the decisions I was trying to skirt around. Because that was true—those decisions were part of my stuff, and I didn't own them. I realized my only course of action was to apologize to the organization and let them know that I was one of "them." Not one of my best moments, but a very real one.

That moment changed how I thought about how I did my job. Maybe there'd be a day ahead when I'd be CEO of an enterprise like this and would have the final sign-off on these large decisions, but that day wasn't today.

My current job meant the privilege and responsibility of serving on the senior team in a company I'd chosen to work for—so with that in mind, I needed to own our decisions as mine, once they were final. In other words, I needed to own my stuff.

Getting Real about your business starts with accountability. Own your stuff. And if not you, who? If not now, when?

What you will become is a direct derivative of your work right now

After P&G and a five-year stint with Sprint, I became co-owner of MAI, a small sports marketing agency based in Kansas City. The work I had was small potatoes compared to my previous jobs: revenues of $3 million, 30 customers, 25 employees. I'd just come from not one, but two Fortune 500s, and believe me, the numbers I've just quoted would not have made an impression in any job interviews for those companies.

Plus, some of the people to whom I was selling our agency services had actually been former employees of mine when I worked at Sprint. Previously, their success depended to a degree on what I thought of them; now my success depended on what they thought of me.

How's that for a situation that could have tempted me to live every day for what might be ahead, rather than what was before me right then?

Fortunately I'd already had a lot of time to practice "own your stuff" thinking, so it was almost knee-jerk for me to take ownership of what was right in front of me. We went to work. We sold. We serviced our clients. We grew into a successful agency that was named the Business of the Year in 1998 by the Greater Kansas City Chamber of Commerce (the Mr. K award winner!).

A couple of jobs later, I found myself back in the world of big business, leading the consumer organization for a telecom company. Now $3 million in revenue had become $2.6 billion, while 30 customers had exploded to 4 million. Instead of 25 employees my organization had over 3,000.

However, in this new, much larger organization, my comfort and success lay in simply doing what I had learned to do in my previous roles, including at the (relatively) small marketing agency, MAI.

The leadership methods, the business development thinking, and the capacity to clear-mindedly prioritize it all were strategies that made sense and were successful with small or large companies or organizations.

There's no quicker way to understand the concept of budget priorities than to have to decide whether to replace a worn-out copier or meet payroll that week. In larger companies the simple beauty of an immediate consequence rarely gets felt so sharply.

However, once the prioritizing principle gets set, it doesn't really change when the stakes get much higher.

If I hadn't given myself without reservation to growing MAI as if it would be my last and only job, I'd have missed critical learning that got me ready to lead an organization with revenues nearly 900 times larger.

Replace "garbage dump" reporting with solution-focused reporting

What happens when your team members make progress reports, especially when they involve bad news? Do you find yourself on the ugly side of garbage dump reports?

You know what I mean. You hear, "This is wrong; that isn't working; this is a problem. Now, Boss Person, what are you going to do about it?"

The reports I'm looking for sound more like this: "This is wrong; that isn't working; this is a problem. So, here are some possible solutions."

"From what I know now, I'd recommend the second solution; here's my thinking. How do you see this? Is there something I'm missing?"

Ownership may mean cleaning up others' messes

It's a powerful experience when you find yourself facing a mess you didn't create. You claim it anyway and commit to dealing with it with as much determination as if you had made it.

In college, my wife Kris worked at a retail jewelry store part time. One November she made several large sales to customers who used their store charge cards to take advantage of the offer she told them about—six months deferred payment with no interest.

Six months later one of her customers called the store. They had received their bill—with $400 in interest charges. My wife had been told that the offer ran through the month of November, when in fact it ended on Thanksgiving Day.

Kris's manager advised her to just wait and see who else called to complain—but she decided to own her stuff. She searched manually through the store's paper receipts to find transactions with her employee number, charged to a store card between Thanksgiving and the end of the month. Then she checked to see which of these still had balances.

There were four, and she called each customer to explain, apologize, and assure them it would be resolved. She then approached her district manager and asked him to call the credit center and clear the interest charges, realizing she could be fired or held accountable financially.

As it turned out, neither negative consequence happened, but Kris didn't know that when she made the decision. Being truly accountable, truly "stepping up," means we take risks like this simply because they're the right thing to do. They're right for employees and right for us as leaders.

Step up. Own your stuff and help your people own their stuff. The mutual trust that will result is key to a Get-Real organization.

9

Measure Up

- Teach them to love competing
- Don't let competing turn cutthroat

Make a game of competing

Life is not like spring training in major league baseball; we're playing the regular season. Whether we like it or not, there is a scoreboard and we are measured. Thus, my mantra is to always compete. I say, if there isn't a scoreboard, the game doesn't matter.

So, I work hard to make a constant game of sharpening my skills at competing.

For over 15 years I timed myself to work every day.

I gave myself the choice of several routes, and I didn't go more than five mph over the speed limit—but other than that, it was *game on* every morning.

I would get in my car, set my stop watch and hit go. Once I hit the parking spot at work, I'd check my watch and hope for a new record time. You'd know it had happened if I jumped out of my car and spiked my briefcase. Yes!

This daily competition was so much a part of me that most employees could tell you I'd cut my best time from 9 min and 13 seconds to 8 minutes and 27 seconds on the four-and-a-half mile drive. When I did an All-Hands webcast, I was often asked, "Have you beaten your time to work?" I still get the occasional Facebook question from a former co-worker wondering if I have a new job and, if so, what's been my best time to work!

I love to compete. I believe healthy organizations are highly competitive organizations, so long as we all define winning as measuring up to the absolute best we can be, rather than winning by dragging others down.

Know your products and your competition

The starting point for scoring higher has to be knowing both your product and competition inside and out.

When I was the brand manager of Metamucil, I knew my distribution channels, key customers, product attributes, etc., better than anyone. Also, I knew the other guys, particularly Ex-Lax and Citrucel, extremely well. I knew more about constipation than anybody you will ever meet and why Metamucil was the best solution. I expected my team to want to be constipation experts, too. Seriously. We couldn't win if we didn't know our solution and why and how it was good enough to be a customer's first choice.

Plus, I expected the team to really know not just the other products, but the other companies we competed against, just as I did. What was their business model? How was it the same or different from ours? How did they market? What was working for them we might learn from?

Your team needs a spirit of competition

Tim Donahue, former CEO of Nextel, showed me how to use competitiveness to energize a team. When Donahue spoke about Nextel's major competitor Verizon, he'd consistently refer to "those litigious SOB's" and what Nextel was going to do to beat them.

I could see he'd crafted a rallying cry, crude though it was, that gave his people an external focus.

Donahue had effectively marshaled the power of a Common Enemy in a slogan that was simple, externally-focused, and authentic. The Nextel employees responded enthusiastically to this style and message and drove hard to be wildly successful.

I decided to follow his example. In our wire-line telecom world, our major competitors were part of the cable industry. Customers went to them initially for cable TV services and found out they could get telephone services, too. The package deal was hard to resist.

So our war cry became, "KCA: Kick Cable's Ass." Common enemy, external focus, simple slogan.

I introduced it in an All-Hands, and it caught on like wildfire. Soon I saw employees walking around our buildings sporting big green KCA buttons.

Of course there was considerable pushback on this one. Should we be saying "ass" in the workplace? What would our moms think? HR pushed us to change those asses to "butts," and others insisted we call it "Kick Cable's A**."

In reality, the conversations that followed only made this rallying cry more fun and more visible. Notice the conversations weren't about whether or not we really should sink Cable's ship—it was only about what words we used to describe how badly we intended to beat them.

Now, this is the way competitive people disagree: over verbiage, never over outcome.

From my view, Mission Accomplished.

Plus, this simply stated external focus provided a clear model for decision-making. Will this decision help us in our efforts to kick Cable's rear end? Then let's do it. If not, why are we doing it? This is the focus I knew could make us winners, and a pushy slogan helped bring it alive.

Keep it light

I often tell competition-based stories about my family, because it keeps this quality in the right perspective.

For instance, my family does a lot of bowling. When my daughter was younger, she got to use gutter bumpers to keep the ball rolling down the alley. As a result, she could throw the ball anywhere on the lane; it would bang off the bumpers on both sides, then invariably knock a bunch of pins down. With the assistance of those bumpers, she beat me regularly.

However, I told her she should savor those victories, because when she turned twelve, the bumpers were coming off, and we'd be going head-to-head on open lanes. We even made a date for her twelfth birthday to inaugurate the new bowling system.

Sure enough, the bumpers came off and I beat her.

Should I have competed with my daughter like this? I say yes! And I tell my people yes. I didn't make her compete without the bumpers when she was little—that wouldn't have been fair, and I'm out to win fairly. But I want her to know I believe she can compete with me.

And you wait. There will be a day when she takes me. But when she does, it will mean something because she'll know I gave her a great run.

Plus, when things get hairy at work, and our wins and losses have bigger implications than a bowling score, stories like this help keep us anchored. What we are dealing with is not life or death, and we should compete fairly.

Keep the focus in the right place

You and your people only have so much energy. You can spend it on internal "stuff"—like gossip or office politics or ballyhooing over arcane policies—or externally on winning.

Now, I'll grant there will be some energy spent on internal stuff, but if you keep it to 5-10 percent of your time and effort, you can spend the other 90-95 percent externally, and win big. The percentage spent internally won't go to zero—we're human, after all!

As the leader, you may find you need to give more of your time to internal stuff so your people can focus externally. A few years ago I wound up spending more hours than I care to count hassling with an overlapping bonus structure that created ambiguity about whether the people in my division would get 80 or 94 percent of their annual bonus.

I cared about the answer as it related to my bonus, but, more importantly, thousands of people in my division would be affected significantly by the outcome! I knew that if I didn't resolve this issue quickly, my goal of keeping internal focus to 5-10 percent would quickly be meaningless—my people wouldn't be able to focus and our results would suffer.

In these cases, the quicker you roll up your sleeves and address internal issues, the easier you make it for your people to do real work that impacts your customers and bottom line. That's what serving your employees means.

Healthy Competition

I like to hold up one of my teenage son's friends to my people as an example of doing competitiveness right. This teenager got a job as a checker at a local grocery. Instead of plugging people through the check-out line while he daydreamed about the weekend, he decided to set up a competition—with himself.

Every day he got a little faster and more accurate than he was the day before. Because there's a scoreboard, and he's competing, he's continually looking for ways to get better, and paying attention to others who do it better, and pushing himself to learn and produce.

The cool thing is that this attitude rubbed off on my son. When he got his first job as a food runner for a local restaurant, he threw himself into learning the menu, the names of the other employees, the table layout, and the process of closing the restaurant at night. Knowing these things made him much better at his job and will serve him well in the future when he starts other jobs.

Now, there are two kids who will do well no matter what life path they choose because they found a way to incent their own improvement. They didn't need a contest or a gimmick or a prize. And they didn't need to cheat or put down anyone else to win at this game.

As a result, they'll win, but their teams and their employers will win, too.

It's models like that that let me remind my people that we're not competing internally—we're competing together to beat external competition.

How do you know if you are competing appropriately? I ask these questions:

- Did you follow the rules?
- How did you act when you won?
- How did you act when you lost?

Bring a strong, competitive energy to your life and your business. Doing it appropriately will generate consistent wins and a whole lot of fun along the way for you and for your people.

10

Change It Up

- Know when you need to change
- Decide for a change!

Use constant learning to drive change

The magic of being a change agent rests mostly in being on a relentless hunt to learn new things. It's not more complex than that. As you continue to learn like crazy, better ways to do things surface more quickly to you than to others.

This bent toward relentless learning can be nurtured, and I'm constantly at it. If you sat next to me at a restaurant, some of my conversation would make you shake your head.

I look around and start asking, "How does this operation work?" I wonder about how they determined the number of wait staff. Why do these hours of operation work for them? Who else serves these menu items, and how do they differentiate themselves?

I have no intention of opening a restaurant. However, these venues are daily life for me, so they provide a good learning lab to keep my observational skills sharp. I love business and believe that asking questions like this help my kids learn to think like businesspeople, too.

If you are an incessant question-asker, keep it up. Curiosity may not directly affect your job performance today, but it could make a huge difference for your company or your organization or your boss over time. By paying attention to how things work around you, you will be more likely to add value to a wide range of problems that need to be addressed.

Figure out how your specific job is connected to other roles in the organization. If you are supposed to sell, sell like hell. However, also ask yourself, how does the marketing operation fit with sales? What happens in the operations group? What are you doing that directly or indirectly affects other groups?

Those connections and the learning they generate will keep you aware of when and how changes need to be made.

Create a change-ready organization

Sometimes flexibility and innovation come from more than attitude. It may also require policy or structural changes in your organization.

For example, in response to employees' requests, we decided to shift a long-standing policy in the call centers at Embarq and allow reps to do personal texts and instant messaging *while* they were talking to customers on the phone.

If you are 25 or under, what I just said may not seem in the least remarkable. But for many leaders in our organization, the idea that employees could be texting a family member at the same time they handled a customer's issue seems totally impossible. However, we had hired folks who practically grew up with electronics as a way of life. Normal for them was studying with the TV on, an iPod plugged in their ears, and two or three instant message conversations going on—all at the same time. For them, to *only* be talking to a customer while texting seemed quiet. It seemed to me they had a case for this change.

However, this is a business, so we measured the effect of the decision.

The service and sales metrics were just as good after this change and our employee turnover dropped dramatically.

This was a huge win for us since the cost of replacing a call center representative was very high when you count recruiting, training and ramp up time. This was a win that wouldn't have taken place if we had not been open to—even *looking for*—innovative ways to improve.

Our ability to adapt to change needs constant refueling. When I interview, I often ask candidates about the changes they've influenced in the groups they've been a part of. I'm not interested simply in their business experiences. Organizations like sororities or fraternities, not-for-profits, and sports teams all provide great opportunities to drive change and lead.

People with an eye out for changing things for the better and the ability to motivate others to change along with them are worth their weight in gold. We need to be on the lookout for them and then make our organizations a place where they can thrive.

Honor your commitments to change

I'd be remiss if I didn't tell you the back story of the instant messaging initiative. The idea was actually generated—and implemented without my knowledge— because I told my people I wanted them to do things I didn't know about.

My intention was empowerment. Our organization was too heavily weighted, in my book, toward checking through, checking up, and checking down before moving ahead. I wanted managers to feel more ownership of their own areas and know that I'd support them. I figured the outcome would be faster decision-making, more accountability, and a more nimble, competitive business.

Well, fine. But honestly, when I heard about this change that allowed instant messaging while on the phone to customers, my knees buckled. I'm guessing my reaction was somewhat generational—I didn't grow up in this multitasking age, so the idea that our reps could do these things while managing customers well wasn't evident to me. Indeed, my bias was probably in the opposite direction.

However, managers took me at my word when I challenged them to improve the business by doing things I didn't know about. And as it turned out, in measurements ninety days after the new policy was put into place, employee retention was much better while customer satisfaction and sales remained strong.

My point is this: when you commit to change, keep your commitment, even if you're nervous.

Deciding to commit will keep you appropriately careful about what changes to install, but you'll also find your employees constantly surprising you with their accountability and business acumen.

Don't get trapped in the paralysis of analysis

As a leader who listens, there will be times when you move more slowly than others to make decisions. It makes sense, doesn't it? You believe the people on your team know things—all the information available does not reside between your ears. You know that asking them and listening carefully to their answers, even their debates and pushback, is going to generate a better conclusion.

But there comes a time when you have to simply make the call. That's your job and why your office is bigger than theirs. It's not because you're smarter, but because the final responsibility to keep the business moving rests with you. So, you stop the information-gathering, you close down the discussion, and you decide.

Deciding can be tough when you're fairly sure you don't have all the information you'd like. These calls are not easy, particularly when you have enough experience to know that one more piece of data could move the decision in a different direction.

However, you can decide with confidence even without all the analysis you'd like if you believe one thing:

Excellent execution will trump perfect strategy every time.

And it does. Great execution can make a so-so decision into a great one, just as poor execution can turn the perfect decision into a disaster.

So don't over-analyze or let your people spend too long in analysis or data-collection. You may not only miss a critical opportunity, but you're teaching them that it's this analysis that holds the power, rather than their execution of the plan.

When you decide, commit and don't look back

The process of decision-making can cripple us if we make the same decision over and over and over. That's essentially the definition of second-guessing. I choose, I move, and then I look back to ask, "What if...?" We need to decide, for our own sakes, and more importantly, for our employees' sakes.

One employee told me, "I always felt like you considered my ideas fairly. But in the end, you might agree with me or you might be really clear that my idea needed to be shelved, at least for now."

"You didn't leave me hanging, wondering if my idea would be implemented or not. You didn't try to spare my feelings by not telling me no. You were direct and decisive, so I knew what to work on next."

It's important, too, to not let your team look back. Dissension and disagreement are not the same because they happen at different times.

Disagreement involves discussion and debate prior to a decision being made—I welcome it. We come away with better choices if there's been some push and pull.

Dissension, which comes into play after a decision is made, cannot be tolerated. Post-decision, everyone needs to be onboard and to jump in enthusiastically to implement the decision as if their first choice was the one selected.

Complaining or undermining of authority at this stage leads to major problems.

Be a listening leader, open to ideas and input. But remember, Getting Real in your business means when it's time to change, you change.

When it's time to decide, you decide.

Your people and your business will be better for it.

Get-Real Leadership, or "Get real, Leadership"

Not long ago, I was telling a colleague about this message and how it had led to a book called <u>Get-Real Leadership.</u>

"Wow," she responded. "Now there's a message I'd like to give to the senior team of most every organization I've worked for—'Get real, Leadership!' "

She'd misheard the title, but I later decided that perhaps she hadn't.

The revolution we most need in business today is a move toward honesty, openness, and authenticity. Living truth and sharing truth. In other words, Get-Real Leadership. Real about leading our people, real about leading our business, but most importantly, real about leading our lives.

I believe it can happen because I've seen it work for me. I hope you'll find it works for you.

EPILOGUE

"Learn from yesterday,
live for today,
hope for tomorrow.
The important thing is to not stop questioning."

— **Albert Einstein**

Epilogue:
Get Real in the Here and Now

It's easy to live in the *what's next* world that we think is waiting for us when the current project is finished, or the current quarter has closed, or the next vacation has arrived, or the last kid is off to college.

However, all this focus on tomorrow may be wasted. All we're really sure of is today.

General Gordon Sullivan, who led the U.S. Army through the post-Cold War transformation, liked to tell his people about a Buddhist monk who understood the power of living fully in today, even though today for him meant the monotony of yet another sink full of dirty dishes to wash.

The monk reflected, "If while we are washing dishes, we think only of the cup of tea that awaits us, thus hurrying to get the dishes out of the way as if they were a nuisance, then we are not alive during the time we are washing the dishes."

In other words, if we can't be fully present while we wash the dishes, chances are we won't be fully present in the moment as we drink our tea either.

There's a powerful lesson for us in his wisdom.

In 2004, just before my wife Kris and I celebrated our first wedding anniversary, she was diagnosed with a malignant, inoperable brain tumor. In that one declaration, our picture of our lives, our future and our world shifted. But in another sense, life barely shifted at all. I have to say I'm clearer on the priority of spending time with my family; although, as you know, this was already a life priority for me. Kris chose to leave the corporate world to become an advocate for brain cancer and to have more time for me and my son and daughter.

We now also have a little boy who was born in 2008, who lights up our lives every day. Kris and I plan as though we'll be around for the next 50 years, but we live each day joyously and energetically. Not conflict-free, of course, because we're human, but the conflicts are shorter and handled with less acrimony than I might have shown at another time in life.

The diagnosis doesn't dominate or dictate our daily lives. It simply helps us focus on how we aspired to live all along—one day at a time.

I'm telling you our story because I want you to know Get-Real Leadership isn't a gimmick to me, or a slogan, or even just a business mantra. It's a way to live life that's richer and fuller and more joyful than any made-up version could possibly be.

❖ ❖ ❖ ❖ ❖

Acknowledgments

A whole troop of people made the dream of this book a reality, starting with friends and employees who through the years talked with me about leadership, then said, "Hey! You should write a book about this…"

To each of you, thanks for the consistent, persistent nudges that kept this idea on my radar screen until the time was right to move ahead.

As for the actual product, ghostwriter Maureen Rank drew from a combination of considerable writing experience and her own years in Fortune 500 leadership to demand from me the best I could give. Maureen is awesome!

Rich Zak, who graciously served as my executive assistant during our years at Embarq, helped clarify and focus the message.

My wife Kris and her former book publicity gurus helped pull together the final details, including Mackenzie Miller with her graphic design talents, and Rebecca Schuler with her media and communications expertise.

Finally, cheers to the rambunctious group of friends and colleagues who, over drinks and appetizers, provided the valuable feedback I needed to test the waters with this message.

A different kind of thanks goes to my DeenerFest buddies – a successful but quirky crowd of (mostly) ex-Procter & Gamble friends.

We have been gathering every October for 16 years now to play a little golf, swap stories, drink a lot of beer and keep each other as real as we can during the shifts and turns in life's journey.

Guys, you can't possibly know the positive effect you have had on my life or how much your friendship means to me. Because of you, I will always keep grinding.

❖   ❖   ❖   ❖   ❖

About the Author

Harry S. Campbell is a highly respected speaker on the subject of leadership, and Get-Real Leadership is the philosophy that has guided his successful 25+-year business career.

Known for his high energy, genuine approach and charisma, Harry commands attention and leaves his audiences striving to be the best leaders they can be.

Harry has been a president for two Fortune 500 companies, co-owner of an award-winning small business, CEO/board member of an Internet start-up and founding member of the industry-changing Walmart-P&G Customer Team in Northwest Arkansas.

He has driven exceptional people and business results in a broad range of industries from consumer packaged goods and telecommunications to sports marketing to digital media.

Harry lives with his wife, Kris, and three children in Overland Park, Kansas. He is an avid Indiana Hoosiers fan, an active member in the United Methodist Church of the Resurrection, a fervent supporter of Head for the Cure and is passionate about motivating people to make a positive impact in their lives, businesses and communities.

You can learn more at get-realleadership.com.

GET-REAL LEADERSHIP

Reader Notes on **Get-Real Leadership**

Reader Notes on <u>Get-Real Leadership</u>

GET-REAL LEADERSHIP

get-realleadership.com

Made in the USA
Lexington, KY
27 March 2015